MAGI GIBSON was joint winner of the Scotland on Sunday/Women 2000 Prize for Poetry, and her work has been widely published in literary magazines and anthologies including *Modern Scottish Women Poets* (Canongate), *Scottish Love Poems* (Canongate), *The Edinburgh Book of Twentieth Century Scottish Poetry*, (Edinburgh University Press), and *100 Favourite Scottish Love Poems* (Luath). She has held three Scottish Arts Council Creative Writing Fellowships, one Royal Literary Fund Fellowship, was Writer in Residence with the Gallery of Modern Art in Glasgow, and Reader in Residence with Glasgow Women's Library. She was appointed the first Makar of the City of Stirling in 500 years in 2009. She received a major Scottish Arts Council bursary for her writing, and has taken part in collaborations with composer Sally Beamish and artist Anthony Schrag. Poems have been translated into Polish, Spanish and German and published in the USA, South Africa, Mexico and Australia. She is also a playwright and children's author. An experienced reader and performer, Magi has appeared at most major book and literary festivals in Scotland. She founded and runs the Wild Women Writing Workshops, and lives in Glasgow with comic novelist and performer Ian Macpherson. She has three grown up children.

By the Same Author:

Poetry
Kicking Back, Taranis Books, 1993
Strange Fish (with Helen Lamb), Duende Poetry, 1997
Premier Results (with Brian Whittigham), Neruda Press, 1997
Wild Women of a Certain Age, Chapman, 2000
Graffiti in Red Lipstick, Curly Snake, 2003
Washing Hugh MacDiarmid's Socks, Luath Press, 2017

For Children
Seriously Sassy, Puffin, 2009
Seriously Sassy, Pinch me, I'm Dreaming, Puffin, 2009
Seriously Sassy, Crazy Days, Puffin, 2010

Plays
One Foot in the Cuckoo's Nest (with Ian Macpherson)
BBC Radio 4, 2006
Our Boys, 2016

I Like Your Hat

And I hope you like these poems!

Magi Gibson

MAGI GIBSON

Luath Press Limited

EDINBURGH

www.luath.co.uk

First published 2020

ISBN: 978-1-913025-73-1

The paper used in this book is acid-free, recyclable and
biodegradable. It is made from low-chlorine pulps produced in a
low-energy, low-emission manner from renewable forests.

Printed and bound by
Bell & Bain Ltd., Glasgow

Typeset in 10.5 point Sabon
by Main Point Books, Edinburgh

In memory of Helen Lamb 1956–2017

Contents

Introduction   9

I Like Your Hat   11
Sitting for Joyce   13
Fuck This Shit   15
Menopausal Thunderstorm   18
Glasgow Epiphany   19
Our Boys   21
I will not be bitter   22
Kitchen Sink   24
Letter from the Asylum, 1915   27
Tick Tock   29
Stella, the Muse of Rose Street   30
The Lassie Frae the Mune   31
Warning from an Ex-Muse   34
Patriarchal Conspiracy #153   38
Three Days Till Christmas   39
Dead Women Count   40
Check   41
The President Visits for a Quick Round   43
Bomber Pilot   45
The Hunter   46
When I am an Old Woman   47
Udderly Smooth Udder Cream   50
October in Stephen's Green   51
Mid-flight   54
On Discovering a Poem in a Summer Garden   56
Thistledown   57
Robin   58

War Shadow   59

Slip into the Moment   72

Burial Ground   74

In Winter Sunshine   75

Winter Night   75

Winter Morning   75

Broody Hill   76

Greylag Geese   77

April 2020   78

Pandemonious   79

On the Hospice End of Life Ward   81

Missing   82

She Dares to Walk Where   84

Fear   109

The First Recorded Case   110

George Square, September 2014   112

Since You Left   116

Dream Poetry Reading   117

Notes on Poems   120

Acknowledgements   122

Introduction

WAITING FOR BUSES at cold bus stops. That's what I seem to spend a lot of time doing. Not that I mind, as often in that state of Scottish Zen, instead of the bus coming along, a poem arrives. This is how 'I Like Your Hat', which introduces this collection, showed up. A poem about everyday kindness. 'Glasgow Epiphany', on the other hand, another 'street' poem, followed me home one day. And 'Dream Poetry Reading' – well, we've all been at one of those, haven't we?

Other poems, such as 'Our Boys', 'Dead Women Count', and 'Check' are my howl against a world beset by social injustice and unnecessary violence, my way of saying, I see you, I am bearing witness. I can't imagine writing a collection without some political poems in there.

Amongst all the poems that came and found me, all those that followed me home and tugged at my sleeve and insisted they be written, are two long sequences, 'War Shadow' and 'She dares to walk where'. 'War Shadow' haunted me for a long time. Both my late mother's story and mine, my insights to her experiences can be only fragmentary, as if I am peering into the past through one small window, at events I can never fully comprehend. That said, this is a truthful account of the little she did tell me.

The other long sequence, 'She dares to walk where', tells a story which is not mine. It's a blend of multiple stories other women have told me, mixed with small parts of my own experience, all intertwined to create a narrative poetic truth.

One thing I was never cut out to be was a muse, for a poet or any other artist. This is a scam I've explored in previous collections and I pick it up again here through the lens of the ultimately tragic life of Stella Cartwright, known as 'The Muse of Rose Street'. I rejoice in *The Kitchen Sink*, photos from the early 20th century of Margaret Watkins who lived for decades in Glasgow, and despair at the fate of the immensely talented Camille Claudel.

Sometimes I'm a magpie poet. A bright idea catches my eye and I fly down for a closer look. Sometimes an eagle poet. Circling high. Then swoop. Sometimes an old bloodhound, doggedly on the trail of something that smells 'poem'.

But mostly I'm that woman waiting at a bus stop. In a cold wind. Hoping someone like you will come along and together we'll form a momentary bond of common understanding. Because ultimately, that's what I'd like these poems to do between you, the reader, and me.

And by the way, before you go, I do like your hat!

Magi Gibson
September 2020

I Like Your Hat

At the bus stop where the wind's trying
to kill us, slicing in like a scimitar from Siberia,
a tiny woman is wearing a colourful velvet beret.

She's so small, I see each segment of its circle
sitting on her head like the wheel
of a stained glass window: emerald, sapphire,

saffron, indigo, amber, red. She beams
when I say it's beautiful, tells me its story;
a gift from her daughter years ago,

she deemed it too bright, too loud,
stuffed it in a drawer, out of sight.
And now, her daughter's dead.

Years later, the bus stop on St Vincent Street,
maybe it's the same wind, slicing in
from Siberia, snow and ice spitting

through its sharpened teeth,
a young woman says, 'I love your hat!'
It's a beret of sorts. Mulberry wool.

'Well cool,' she says. 'Unusual.'
'It's from a charity shop,' I reply.
Then she admires my scarf. Hand-woven

in India. Fairtrade. And while the bus
doesn't come, we talk recycling, pollution,
climate change, and I see she's carrying

an art portfolio under one arm, while
on her shoulders she bears the future
of the world. And I swear her smile's

so beautiful, this student girl
I've never met before, she's lighting up
the shelter like an angel in a holy grotto

as all around the drear November dusk
descends black as the wings of ravens.
And the glow from her face warms me

more than my woollen kind-of-beret
or my hand-woven Fairtrade scarf or best
thermal underwear from Marks & Spencer,

or my specially lined duvet coat as worn
by explorers to far Antarctica
guaranteed to keep me warm at minus fifty

in a hurricane. And as we chat I recall
the tiny lady's velvet beret, its jewelled
wheel of colours, and her sadness as she said

she wore it now to please her daughter,
who is dead. And all the while the darkness
deepens as if the sky is leaking sin

and the east wind with its icy breath
from Siberia does its best to kill us
and cut like a scimitar

through the warmth
of our common humanity.

Sitting for Joyce

A morning of spring birth, the sun crowning
after a long confinement, the sky opening its eye,
molten gold pouring through.

I swear you could hear the frozen heart
of the earth crack and fibrillate
as the bus sped the dark line of the M8

from Glasgow to Edinburgh. I hoped for lambs.
Instead a straggle of deer, russet
as winter ferns, grazed a wind-bleached field

with the hard-earned dignity of survivors.
And I thought of us, the white-haired women
who'd endured. And I thought of friends,

left behind in winter's cold.
In Stockbridge, I bought you flowers!
Tulips red, purple, gold.

Tight young blooms on long,
green stems you placed in a white Delft vase.
Later you captured on creamy canvas

their beauty as they stretched and curved
like ballerinas in a painting by Degas.
Soon, their swan necks will droop

with the weight of time, their slender stems
sag, their silken petals open wide before,
exhausted, they will drop.

Yet this image you created will remain,
unchanged. I sat on the love seat in your studio.
You, one hand porcupined with pencils,

the other fluttering like a small industrious dove,
sketched and drew, glittering dust motes gyring
in the air around your wild white hair.

We chatted, shared our tales of wisdom
and of foolishness, as older women do.
Of dreams squandered, dreams fulfilled.

And all the while we laughed and smiled,
giddy and bright as young girls blossoming
because it was spring, and the earth was quickening.

Fuck This Shit

I'm here to meet Jenny in Edinburgh's Old Town,
two poets about to set the world to rights, or
at the very least eat cake. But I'm early, she's late,
and I've committed that schoolgirl poet sin
no notebook to scribble in, no paper scrap, not even
the back of a fag packet, just an Ali Whitelock book
so off I go to look for a cheap little notepad
when I'm sucked into a tartan-on-steroids
tourist shop. *Notebooks! We have notebooks!* the guy
behind the counter grins, waving at rack upon rack –
Monarch of the Glen stares back; kilted men, bare
bums; purple heather, misty weather; mountains,
brooding, sun-lit, moon-lit; Grannie's Hielan' Hame.
Bagpipe muzak zaps my brain, I reel as if trapped
with a drunk in a midnight Strip the Willow.
No thanks, I mutter as I dash through a door
onto the rain-drenched cobbles of Cockburn Street,
where there's a tinge of sanity and a shop that's
more 'boutique'. Okay, so it's a bit young, a bit hip,
and the twenty something assistant dripping
disdain and Hispanic chic with bright
hibiscus blossoms in her hair is daring
me to stay outside – I'm not the wished-for clientele
with my menopausal hint of dull – but what the hell!
I'll tell her I'm shopping for a great grand-niece.
For stacked between the Himalayan Salt
Lamps, hand-carved herbal crystals, Klimts,
Koons and Kahlos I spy notebooks with plain
black spines. A poet's dream! But as I slide
one out, its cover Swarovski-crystal-twinkles
WHAT WOULD BEYONCÉ DO?
I don't have a clue! I put it back, pull another

from the stack. WHEN LIFE GIVES YOU
MONDAY DIP IT IN GLITTER AND
SPARKLE ALL DAY. And all the while
Miss Hispanic Chic tracks my every move
as if I'm a spider, she's an arachnophobe,
and all her scary staring make me feel like
I'm some crazy kleptomaniac even though
I know I'm not, till my skin starts to prickle, and
really I can do without this primal animosity so
full on now the air appears to crackle. What's her
issue anyway? Class? Or age? Is she an alien from a
galaxy called Youth – and Scary Older Women are her
Kryptonite? Quickly I choose some pencils, plain,
that say along one side
FOR WRITING SHIT DOWN.
One for Jenny, one for Ali, one for me,
a notebook
that declares in boldest gold
A WISE WOMAN ONCE SAID
FUCK THIS SHIT
AND SHE LIVED
HAPPILY EVER AFTER.

And as I pay the oh-so-chill girl at the till
she studiously avoids my smile as if
she really thinks one look from me might kill.
Listen, child, I want to say, *excessive frowning*
causes wrinkles; ageing is not contagious,
the crone in many cultures is revered;
and Frida Kahlo with her magnificent brow
staring down all around from block posters,
high gloss trays and mugs and plates and even
a fucking clock with black wire hands twirling
from her nose (and whose look you're trying
so hard to emulate) was born in 1907, *which makes*
her ages with my gran, and they're both dead and cold

in their graves, which is way worse than being OLD,
and if you're very lucky you'll live long enough
to learn this too. Instead I say *Thank you,*
take my notebook and pencils and go
clucking from the shop
to set the world to rights with Jenny
and cake and poetry talk.

Menopausal Thunderstorm

The rain hammers black fists
at the midnight door
the wind howls at the windows
the dog cowers in the corner

Kate throws back a whisky, kicks
off her shoes, strips off her
cardigan, skirt, her cotton
underwear
and fifty years of
prim propriety
runs bare-foot
bare-bum
bare-naked
in the garden
whoops, leaps, dances,
glows and gleams
white body
moon-luminous
under clouds that billow
dark as witches' petticoats

her husband, dumbstruck,
gawks, slack-jawed
at the window, gormless
prince turned glass-eyed toad

a cataclysmic crack
splits
the skies apart

Kate's fingers spark
forked lightning.

Glasgow Epiphany

Underneath the No Waiting
At Any Time sign
where a homeless man's been dossing

in a doorway, someone
has scrawled in white chalk
I CAN SEE INTO YOUR SOUL.

A thought that stalks me
dogged as my own shadow
onto Great Western Road,

past the kebab shop, and the
graffiti-scratched bus stop,
where a drunk is singing

obscenities into the cold ear
of the east wind. I can see
into your soul... seven syllables

that susurrate softly at the fringes
of my consciousness, fluttering
like the soft white wings

of the guardian angel I stopped
believing in when I was eight,
haunting me with whispers

of afterlife and sin and lost souls
with no place to sleep at night. So
when three Jehovah's Witnesses

in the fading winter light offer me
Watchtowers with a sprinkling
of eschatological warnings

at the side door of Òran Mór,
I think maybe it will free me
of the strangeness of it all if I pass

the Good News on that up around
the corner in a dead end street
where No Waiting is Permitted

for All Eternity, there's a down-and-out
dossing on cardboard in a doorway
who can see into their Immortal Souls –

when from the frozen branches
of a black-boughed tree
at the red-amber-green lights

where four roads meet and
the traffic roar stops starts stops,
and you can hardly hear the pound

of your own heartbeat, the song
of a blackbird rises into the city dusk
scattering sparks of stardust

like a tiny resurrection.

Our Boys

They die, you know, left out on nights like this,
sleeping in shop doorways and in ditches,

foetal as uncurled ferns, dew-soaked at dawn.
What will you be when you grow up? That age-old

question tossed their way when they were small,
playful as a bouncing ball. They learned to say:

lawyer, engineer, footballer, rich.
Now, they tease an early morning roll-up

between death-cold fingers. And in the no-jobs-here
Job Centre, plastic potted plants twitch

like dodgy camouflage when they appear,
the fluorescent light flickers its faulty detonator switch,

austerity with government-sanctioned glee aims
a sniper rifle at their foreheads, while battalions

of only-obeying-orders keyboards click   click   click
and the future slams the emergency exits shut.

I will not be bitter

I will not be bitter,
she said out loud
though there was no-one
there to hear.

I will not be bitter
she wrote it out
a thousand times
and cried because
there was no teacher
she could hand it to.

I will not be bitter,
she whispered
in every room
she'd died a little in.

In the kitchen
the fridge cold-shouldered her.
In the bathroom
the mirror eyed her glassily –
it hadn't smiled at her for months.
In the living room
the TV looked blank.

And in the bedroom, the bed,
the traitorous bed
cowered under its duvet –
and would not even offer
a pillow she could cry on.

I will not be bitter, she said
as she snipped her long blonde hair
and stuffed it in the bin.
I will not be bitter, she said
as she torched the lingerie
he'd loved to see her in
and watched her frillies flame.

I will not be bitter, she said
as she stuffed her face with
chocolate fudge ice cream,
and chucked out every single thing
that made her think of him, and
downed a fist of pills
with vodka laced with gin.

I will not be bitter, she slurred
as they pumped her stomach,
hooked her to the intravenous drip.

And when they searched her purse,
and asked if the fellow
in the photograph
was her next of kin, she
raised her head,
said clear and strong,
No! Anyone but him.

And then she knew, at last,
the worst was past –
she'd soon be better.

Kitchen Sink
Margaret Watkins, Photographer, 1919

1.

Growing up in Canada you feared, not
being eaten by a bear, accidentally shot
by hunters gone berserk, or falling through
the jagged ice of a frozen lake, but rather
the horrendous thought of being
'domesticated to death'.

Years later, safe in Greenwich Village,
you took aim at your kitchen sink, caught
the light on its seductive rim, smooth,
creamy as licked-clean bone, zoomed in
on the brass tap's rude protuberance,
its unleashed gush, snapped and trapped
its spumous rush on silver gelatin.

2.

What was in your mind that day you rammed
the wood-stemmed dish-mop in the round
hole of the overflow? Adjusted it to poke
just so, at the rakish angle of a jaunty cock?

Did you know you'd make – a century after –
another woman rock with laughter
at your wicked joke? I like to think you loved
your photographs to shock. I like to think
you said, drawing coolly on a Russian cigarette,
'Why all the fuss? It's just a photo of a kitchen sink.'

3.

This sink's rolled enamel rim, sensuously curved
like a lover's shoulder blade. Three hens' eggs, perfect
ovals on a softly textured cotton towel. A sudden drop.

Those eggs! Brown, off-white, white-not-quite.
Metaphor? For what? The ego of the artist?
Femaleness? Fragility? Or might
they represent the quickly ticking time
bomb of your own fertility?

Such early morning stillness
in this shot, yet...
                    one tug on the dangling
waterfall of cloth and oh
                    this small
                            Domestic Symphony would
slowly roll
            and
                    fall
plop
            plop
                            plop

                                    into that aching

gaping

        hole
                of

                    black

                                    oblivion.

4.

Did you wake one morning, blink bleary at the sight
of unwashed dishes from the night before, sigh –
then in a flashbulb moment think – *there's art
in this! Right here. This kitchen sink!*

Milk bottle, water-filled, scum-topped, a china
cup, an unwashed bowl, rim-chipped, a striped
milk jug, a soaking pastry brush, a… phial?
Why surely that's a witch's implement? And see

that curious kettle spout, curved as an old crone's nose,
peeping in at the photo's edge, gasping at the mess,
while looming on the wall the kettle's shadow, mad
as a fat round moon, an evil twin, rocks with joy

at what one critic, outraged, called this
'celebration of dirty housekeeping'!
And you exhibited at the Annual Salon
as *Still life composition. Kitchen Sink.*

5.

While others sought the mirror of a soulful lake,
the drama of a deep-etched cliff or angry waterfall
to test their skill with this new art, you stayed
inside, calculating shadow, angle, light,
handling silvered plates, fragile negatives,
rocking stop baths, mixing noxious chemicals,
a woman happy in her kitchen after all!

Letter from the Asylum, 1915

What is the reason for this cruelty?...
I would like to know

> Born female. Born ambitious.
> Born talented.

> Born free-thinking and assertive.
> Born a century too soon.

> Answering in a playful questionnaire
> In 1888 when twenty-one:

> Your favourite virtue.
> I don't have any: they're all boring.

> Your favourite qualities in a man.
> To obey his wife.

> Your favourite qualities in woman.
> To make her husband fret.

> Your idea of misery?
> *To be the mother of many children.*

> Your favourite colour and flower.
> *The most changing colour*
> *And the flower which does not change.*

> If not yourself who would you be?
> *A hackney horse in Paris.*

> Your favourite poets.
> *One who does not write verse.*

Your favourite painters and composers.
Myself.

Your favourite food and drink.
Love and fresh water.

What is your present state of mind?
It is too difficult to tell.

Signed, *Camille Claudel.*

Tick Tock

She says: glass. He thinks: fragility. She
says: pretty face. He thinks: lady.

She says: delicate hands. He thinks:
femininity. She says: roses, yellow.

He conjures up a scented garden, birdsong
a summer evening, while she imagines

a sisterhood of Suffragists, blossoming.
She says: cogs and wheels that click and spin

with beautiful efficiency. He thinks: clock!
She says: yes – but no! She's got in mind

a different kind of movement. He fails to grasp
just why this makes her laugh. She wears

the timepiece with its secret message
dangled on a chain between her breasts,

a shiny globe of polished glass
a tiny ticking heartbeat of sedition.

*Written for a lady's watch pendant in Glasgow Women's Library
Archive. A glass globe, the size of a child's marble, its watch face
is painted with yellow roses, the American Suffragist's symbol.
Its back is glass, the cogs and wheels visible.*

Stella, the Muse of Rose Street

Poets gaze at her. Oh, the brightness of this teen,
her golden laugh, her hair! In Milne's Bar, all oak

and smoke and gloom, her father orbits round
his sparkling star, observes his drinking mates ignite

bright as turnip lanterns when she's near. He preens
himself to know this girl whose face illuminates

the dullest room, this girl for whom these men will spill
their pens, this adolescent who incites such passion

with her numinescent glow, is herself a work of art
that sprang from him; his very own creation.

And while she sparkles ever brighter, supping
whiskies down with compliments from poets twice

her age, while with gentleness she carefully unknots
the jingle-jangled tangle of their genius heads,

in distant darkened rooms the great men's wives
tuck their children safely in their beds.

The Lassie Frae the Mune

Googling for her face, the painting
of The Poets' Pub appears,
The Great Men in their Pantheon.

I'm about to scroll on past, when
I think of Stella in that place
of whisky, smoke and myth,

and peering close I see, behind
the Great Men's heads, a painting
in the painting of a fair-haired girl

caught up in a wild embrace.
Strange how half a century ago,
in public life, in art, women seem

an afterthought as if a different breed,
a different race. But wait! What's that?
A real life girl! Half-hidden by the men

of words who dominate. She's balanced,
awkward on a barstool, head drooped,
one leg pretzeled, scarlet-stockinged,

and red-shod, louche as a lush,
one breast exposed – hell, is she nude?
The artist's made her face a blur,

a few sad lines, stuck her there
amongst these men all well-defined
and fully clothed – she doesn't even have

a glass of wine. While just outside
the open door, dressed head to toe
in black, another woman waits.

For what? Is she a whore?
Oh Stella! Sweet teen
from a genteel neighbourhood.

Is this the kind of company you kept?
A lassie 'built for love' one poet said.
'Life giver', said another. Countless claimed

you as their muse or lover. You,
with your patience and your voice
'of roses and rain'.

The poet with the salt seas tiding
in his veins praised the gentleness
he found in you, said you were

more sinned against than sinning.
He loved you once, though pulled
like a magnet to the northern island

of his birth, he left you too. While you
stayed here, and never truly took
the time to find the art within yourself.

You gave that gift, and more, to careless men.
And then there was 'the smiler with the knife'
you never could turn down – Jock Barleycorn.

Those women in the Poets' Pub. I look
at them again. Ach, sisters! What an unjust
world that bade you play the whore,

the nurse, the listener, the muse, to keep
afloat that fragile craft, that flimsy boat,
that was your life. While for their part,

the poets drank their whiskies, wrote
their verse, took centre-stage, as seemed
their right and heritage – and made their art.

Warning From an Ex-Muse

i.m. Camille Claudel

Listen, sister, this is how it starts.
He says he finds your work 'of note'.

And you, much more mature
than all your mates – those giggling

air-head girls! Soon he'll suggest
you meet at launches, bookshops,

galleries, for coffee and a chat. On art.
He's erudite. He knows that you 'aspire'.

He's keen to cultivate. He says he sees
his younger self in you. So,

how about a little dinner date?
Your friends will say he's old.

And odd. And hasn't he a 'wife' at home?
But, oh my god. What charm!

And as you swoon and preen
and wonder what to wear you think,

Hey – what's the harm?
But sister – do beware!

This is how he sets the snare.
Soon his needs will escalate.

He'll say he needs your presence
by his side so he can work. He'll claim

you are his inspiration! And should you
say you'd rather not, you've got

your own career to grow –
he'll drag a grand piano

through the streets, dress in a tuxedo,
rattle out concertos, lit by the glow

of a midnight moon beneath
the window where you sleep.

And should you text next day to say,
um, no that's not the deal, you'd really

rather be alone, you need a break, it's
all too much, too fast, too soon

he'll hire a plane, fly loop-de-loop,
scribe your name across the cerulean

summer sky, dot it with heart-shaped clouds
he's crafted from the wool of living sheep

he sheared himself. This man will promise you
the golden apples of the moon,

the silver apples of the sun,
baked in a filo pastry drizzled

with ambrosia he's milked
from the teats of ancient goddesses.

He'll give you ANYTHING
you ask, he'll pop it in a contract,

write it in invisible ink
only poets use. If only

you – it must be you! –
will be his muse.

He'll make you sign the contract
with your blood.

He'll seal it in an envelope
of your skin.

He'll call it Art.
AN INSTALLATION!

He'll light you up in neon
display you, gently bleeding

(for that's what women do)
in an exhibition, win

A PRESTIGIOUS PRIZE!
(though strangely you won't get a mention)

THIS IS WHAT IT MEANS
TO BE A MUSE.

He is the vampire,
you the blood.

You are the water bubbling
from the mountain, the flowing

river of ideas, the living fountain
where The Great Man

gulps his inspiration.
You are the dam that powers

his failing turbine.
The steam that pumps his piston.

You are the lightning
life force of creation.

And every now and then
you will be the moonlit lake

he'll kneel before to weep
at the ravaged beauty of

his own reflection.
So sister, heed this warning!

Sign that contract... and you'll
sign away your art.

Sign it, and you'll sign away
your living, beating heart.

Patriarchal Conspiracy #153

when I type in
FEMINIST
it autocorrects

now my T-shirt reads

THIS IS WHAT
A
FANTASIST
LOOKS LIKE

Three Days Till Christmas

in the packed department store,
shoppers laden like sherpas

trek through forests
of synthetic trees,

wade through drifts
of special offers.

in the midst of this throng
under twinkling tinfoil stars

she wanders alone
on sandalled feet

donkey-brown coat
buttoned up all wrong

perched upon her unbrushed hair
a crown of tinsel thorn.

crowds part before her
like a red sea miracle.

she floats by on a cloud
of cheap whisky.

while her voice soars above
the festive ringing of cash registers.

a fallen angel singing
in the bleak midwinter.

Dead Women Count

She counts dead women. Not women
wiped out in warzones by bullets and bombs, nor

the 63 million missing in India – Rita Banjeri
is keeping count of them. Nor is she counting

the Korean Comfort Women, piecing
together what's left of their bones

from the fire pits where they perished. No,
she keeps count closer to home. But not

the victims of wild-eyed strangers they drilled
us to evade: *stay with your pals when you leave the pub,*

don't walk down darkened lanes, don't take shortcuts
through woods alone, don't get into vans,

don't wear too short skirts, too high heels,
low-cut tops, don't end up a headline,

a corpse, a break-a-mother's-heart statistic,
in a ditch. No, not those! She is counting women

killed with knives, shotguns, ropes, with septic
tanks and fists, with poison, cricket bats and fire

each killed by a man who said he loved her once,
a boyfriend, husband, partner, ex, a man she trusted

in her home. A man who thought her life no longer
counts. But she is counting, every week, every one.

And we are counting with her.

Check

Please check you have ticked
all the relevant boxes
before you hand in your life.

Check you have all your loved ones
neatly stored in the locker
above your head.

Check you have fastened your
seat belt. Check your children's hair
for nits, their brains for bigotry.

Please check under the sink for
your darkest thoughts
the ones with the safety tops

marked TOXIC
dangerous to think.
Should they leak, turn your

conscience over like a stone
watch the evil that is in you
scurry from the light.

Please check you have your
ticket for this flight.
Check your destination

country of origin, birthright.
Thank your lucky stars
this is not a police state. Yet.

Please check your breasts
once a month. Check your mattress
for house dust mites. Check

your vagina for thrush
singing or otherwise.
Check your heart for signs of

hardening, your brain for signs
of softening. Check your conscience
for midge bites, these may cause

itching at night, easily mistaken
as guilt. Carry a clipboard and pen
wear an officious frown

stop people in the street, check
their sexual orientation, politics,
class, race, religion, age.

And where appropriate –
check your rage.
But most of all oh most of all,

grip that internal clipboard tight and
check   check   check
your privilege.

The President Visits for a Quick Round

And when he lands, demand the laces
from his shoes. Make him descend

the steps of Air Force One, brogues
flip-flopping, watch as he shuffles

in the effort not to trip. On the tarmac whip
the belt from his golfing trews, try not

to smile as he clasps them as they slip,
check through his papers at the passport gate,

flick the pages, stroke your chin and frown,
suck air in noisily through pursed lips, tap

on your computer screen, silently stride off, return,
scrutinise him head to toe as if the very sight

would make you spew, strip him of his dignity,
crumple and toss it in a bin just beyond

his reach, then separate him
from his startled wife, bundle him along

a corridor, lights flickering, through
an armour-plated door marked ALIEN.

Incarcerate him in a cage. Wrap him in tinfoil.
Tell him to wait; his case has been referred

for further, full investigation. No discussion
can be entered into. Due process will be followed.

And no! No reasons need be given. He
is our guest now. Oh, and – fáilte!

Did we say fáilte? Welcome.

Bomber Pilot

Fresh-in from Afghanistan
she poses pretty as an angel
for the TV crew.

Tanned and blonde
her grin broad as America
she tells the folks back home
she's proud she's fighting
for World Peace.

Smiling still, she turns,
marks another notch
on the ammunition hatch.

But when she falls asleep tonight
will she dream of glory days
and apple pie?

Or will she plummet deep
to where another woman holds
a shattered future to her breast

beneath a blazing sky

The Hunter

only kills for the table, he says

the table shifts uneasy
on its four stout legs

a shadow drifts across
its polished face

as it wonders
what will be put on it next

When I am an Old Woman

When I am an old woman, I shall wear
beige – a bloodless, weary colour.
I'll let my hair turn grey and wispy
as a winter's day. I'll keep myself
to myself, flicking idly through
my memories, chuckling at my wanton
youth, the wildness of my middle years,
the manic madness of my many marriages.

When I am an old, old woman
I shall rarely go out in the rain
for fear of shrinkage, and sudden
disappearance down a gushing drain.

On dry days, I'll wrap up sensibly
and venture forth to gather
from my garden the lost footballs
of the neighbours' children.
Quietly and with dignity I will
stab them with my kitchen knife.

When I am a tiny, twisted pretzel
of a very old woman, I'll have
a walking frame, a flowery cane
and a tartan shopping trolley.
I'll make a game of tripping
up young mothers with impossibly
cheery, cherub-cheeked children.
I will lean my hook-nosed, bird's nest
head into their prams and oooh
and aahhh, and quietly nip
the sleeping babes then tut
my disapproval at their wailing.

Oh really I can't wait to be old!
I'll wear big comfy knickers
and wrinkly support tights
and zimmer-waltz past building sites
ogling the rippling muscles of young men,
I'll wolf-whistle and shout, Get 'em out
for the girls! while I lurk safe
beneath my magic cloak
of ancient crone invisibility!

I'll moan loud and long
about wandering wombs
when the bloke next to me
on the train man-spreads;
I'll dunk my custard cream
when the social worker calls,
and if he's woke and beardy
with a pronoun badge
I'll slurp my soup, witter winningly
about my hot and messy multiple
love affairs. Oh how hard it was
back then, my dear, I'll patiently explain,
one never knew if one was hetero,
lesbian or just plain bi. One simply
had to try, try, try again! You young folk
nowadays have it easy
with all this gender fluid guff,
we hippies only had Free Love!

When I am a spritely and antiquacious
elderly lady with a hearing aid
I'll sprinkle my chat with
bastard fuck and fuckity cunt
like glitter on a Pride Parade.
I'll cheerily smoke pot/grass/weed/
whatever comes my way,
and chomp my gums. But –

if ever, ever that day comes
when I want to wear
PURPLE
shove me in a home without delay,
and with my blessing,
throw the key away.

Udderly Smooth Udder Cream
GOLD STANDARD BIG VALUE EXTRA LARGE JAR

Amazon Review

Having applied the udder cream
to various parts of the body,
I can confirm the burn was

quite phenomenal.
This 'tingle' manifested itself
in particular on the eye

and testicle area, though
the nipples did produce
a satisfying sensation

lasting for hours
that its Original Source
would struggle to replicate.

I would not recommend
this product for the groin
or anus region.

The burn was sensational.
The fact it's toxic to
aquatic life is
also a concern.

One star ✶

October in Stephen's Green

On the humpy-backit bridge we take a seat,
its grey stone polished to a marble sheen
by a thousand elbows and arses. Around our feet
the pond ducks dawdle-waddle – no need to rush

when slabs of plush white bread float uncontested.
Even the slice so generously spread
with chocolate paste does not incite a crush
as city ducks float by, well-fed.

*

A woman drifts past in a faint flip-flap
of soft long skirt. A grey suit dashes by,
his fingers jingling keys – a covert rosary
deep in his troubled pocket. Across the sky

a jet plane streaks a white trail like a slug.
Men with dark briefcases, darker thoughts, lug
documents and files, and secret sandwiches.
Three pigeons strut clawed vermilion feet

across the leaf-strewn lawns as pale-faced
office workers settle down on warm park benches.
Girls' voices chatter past like shifting stones,
the fountain spouts parabolas of glistening sibilants,

the urban young clutch mobile phones;
illuminated amulets to scare off loneliness.
Hanged Mary haunts the shadows
in her stolen dress.

*

The wind has blown the red-eyed aborigine
who last week busked in Grafton Street
out of his tribal skins and beads
into jeans, a fleecy top, a knitted hat.

He's ditched his didgeridoo
in his stuffy rented flat, yet still
his Guinness coloured skin,
his hands that swoop and dive like gulls
entrance the native girls, while he regales
with shaman-speak and outback tales.

*

Black-clad, stealthy as a deathwatch beetle,
the park-keeper creeps through bush and nettle,
walkie-talkie slung low at hip, sharp-eyed,
mean-faced, slim-thighed, lean-lipped.

Like a lawman from a cowboy film, he hunts
the villain and his lass, lewd and libidinous
in the grass, a druggie or a down-and-out,
a wino, drunk or litter lout

so he can stage a shoot-it-out

*

The man with the black beret, the blondish tuft
of ponytail, the greying furze about his chin
stops beside the black-lined bin, stares into
its plastic depths, thrusts his veined hand in,
fishes out a bashed Coke can, twists
it in his weathered fist –
hunter-gatherer of aluminium
green and urban activist.

*

Three women cast in bronze, three Fates
guard one entrance to this park; blind-eyed
they do not see the child the doting dad
has brought out for a walk – a tiny toddler
tottering in red and shiny shoes, her small hand
scattering crumbs for hens who scratch and squawk.

Nor do the City Fathers choose to see
the shadowy figure in the dark, waiting
for the child he fathered on a sink estate.
Shivering in the midnight wind, she
sells her body by the tall park gate.

Mid-flight

For Helen

While we sat, chatting, laughing, (oh how we loved
to laugh! Uproariously!) sipping tea, strong and black
(remember, you were always short of milk)

a sudden, deafening thwack against the glass
stopped us short. We turned. Shocked. What
did we expect? Perhaps a bullet hole? A jagged brick?

The window crazy-cracked in cartoon-style zig-zags?
But what we saw was – nothingness. Stock still,
ears pricked, senses on alert we sat. And in that

eerie quiet, nothing could explain just what
had brought our easy chatter to that stop.
No shout outside. No scream. No vandal's

running feet. Nothing to be seen across the quiet
fields. Till slowly on the windowpane
a shadow-bird, so faint at first it seemed imagination

or a dream, feathers delicately etched, ghosted
wings outspread, soft outline of head, brief hook
of beak marking where, full of energy and life,

the sparrow hawk and death collided with such
sudden cruelty, mid-flight. And then, that afternoon
in early spring, when I sat reading in a sunny room

– the phone's persistent ring, the distant crackling
disembodied voice, explaining that they'd found
you, sitting at your desk. And you were gone.

They had to say it over. Over. Even then, I couldn't
take it in. You, my life-long friend, I'd laughed
with days before, so full of dreams and plans,

no sign of being ill. Taken, sudden,
as the sparrow hawk mid-flight.
I sat there stunned. I am stunned still.

On Discovering a Poem in a Summer Garden

A short black line
as if a careful pencil
made a score

or the dash of an
exclamation mark
took fright

leapt by magic
to this topmost knife-edge
edge of printed page.

It sits stock still. Now
unfolds legs, needle thin,
stretches, genuflects,

becomes
a micro-dancing
insect balanced on

a makeshift stage,
opens fragile wings
shimmering, delicate

filtering sunlight
through finest filigree –
more poem on this page

than words I write
when with a breath
of summer breeze

it lifts in flight and

vanishes from sight.

Thistledown

I still have the thistledown
that tangled in my hair
the day we lay together
on the high moor.

I combed it out
kept it in an envelope.

I combed out kisses too.
I've kept them all this time
in the envelope of my heart.

Why don't you come by soon,
collect what's yours?

Robin

on a white pillow of puffed up snow
the robin's breast
pulses red, fast
as my heart
when i
think
of
you

War Shadow

I am a child of shadows and silences,
of unspoken stories, born

into a house too small for the living,
where ghosts shift restlessly.

By day my mother pushed my pram
over soot-dark cobbled streets,

hung out washing on the line,
all the time the hum of a war plane

thrumming in her head,
its shadow, wings outspread,

blocking out the sun, while
beneath the glinting glass

in its rear-gunner's bubble,
the man she loved, hunched

in terror and alone, gripped
his machine gun as he strafed

the past with hot red streaks
of pain, willing her to run

run   run   run   into the safety
of the future, to leave

all memory of him behind
to live her life, and love again.

*

Ghosts leave clues. Not finger- or foot-prints,
they're far too worldly-wise for that. Ghosts

haunt the cracks where past and present
don't quite meet; scattering

small signals – sudden chills, the distant
pitter-pattering of feet, a soft white feather

lighting on the sill. And children, loving
mysteries, eyes wide as magnifying glasses,

ears alert to the tiniest of creaks, are
natural detectives. We hear her

small sighs as she chops the carrots
for the soup; the melancholy in her voice,

singing *Que sera, sera* on washing day,
we see her elbow-deep in sorrow

soft as suds; we sense a loss that time
won't wash away. And soon, on

playful raids to our parents' room –
we know is out of bounds –

we unearth treasures hidden deep, things
we've never seen her wear;

a gold engagement ring, tiny diamonds
in a pattern like a flower, stored

in a box of shimmering pinks and greens
pretty as a sea-shore shell; a necklace

formed from beads of glass that held
in sunlight scatter rainbows on our skin;

a soft silk scarf sensuous to touch; and
way below her winter woollens, tucked

well back, a stack of letters, pastel blue,
fragile as the wings of long-dead butterflies,

addressed to a name we do not know
our mother by. And buried separate,

stiff and cold, our small hands excavate
a Telegram. War Office. June 6th 1944.

WE DEEPLY REGRET TO INFORM YOU
YOUR HUSBAND IS MISSING IN ACTION

Is this the reason for our mother's silences,
her secret sadness, what she's grieving for?

*

She kept him on the sideboard
in a square of glass she polished.

To us he only ever was a stranger
from another time, another place;

film star looks, airman's uniform,
neat brown hair, the bluest eyes,

more blue even than my favourite doll.
Our father said he was an uncle,

his name was Peter, like my brother,
his plane was shot down in the war.

Uncles, we knew, were grown up men
we were related to. We did not touch

the photograph, did not probe or ask
too much, the way we did not poke

our fingers into bleeding cuts.
Small as we were, we understood

that even when skin heals and forms
a scab, underneath the cut's still raw,

it weeps, the wound still hurts.

*

Nestled on my mother's lap, flicking
picture books, or after lunch, giggling

at the Flower Pot Men, I loved to twist
and turn her wedding rings.

Two gold bands. Because, she said,
(when I was old enough to understand)

she was twice wed. Once to my dad,
once to the blue-eyed man, the man

in the photograph, the man now dead.
Gold is soft. Gold rubs gold.

Slowly, surely down the years
one love rubs away the other.

Each ring grows thin and thinner.
Until one shears.

And disappears.

          *

You are in your teens before
she feels that yes, she can reveal

there is a wound, she bears
a hurt, that something

awful happened in the war.
'The night before,' she says,

'was sunny, warm. Out with my mum,
we strolled across the farmer's field,

a mile or so from home,
a herd of cattle charged.

We dashed together for the gate.
My mother stumbled, fell, near

passed out with the fright
of all those heifers hammering

across the grass, grunting,
snorting. Wild, as if we posed

some kind of threat.' History
would record what happened

over France that night, a thousand
miles away, as Operation Overlord.

'How beautiful the evening was,'
she says, 'before the cattle spooked.

The hedgerows green and lush,
in the air the clear notes of a thrush.

The following day, the neighbour's boy
came running to my work,

red-cheeked, out of breath;
to fetch me home without delay.

He couldn't say just why. I asked
my boss to get away, ripped off

my lab coat, rushed out for a bus,
heart thumping in my chest, fearful

all the way, worst case scenarios
spinning in my head; had my mother

– never strong – been taken ill –
a heart attack? a stroke? or worse?

I feared she might be dead –
Instead, I found her pacing

pale-faced at the door,
in her hand The Telegram.

That was how I heard.'

*

She waits until you happily
announce your pregnancy – another

ten years on – to open up the wet
mouth of her wound again.

'You'll need to know –' She glances
at my belly, barely curved, yet filled

with so much hope.
'I once gave birth to twins.

In wartime. Long before you three were born.'
She turns her back, heats the teapot

for the tea. And you sit still, as if
a bomb's been placed onto your lap.

You hold your breath, don't move,
in case a careless word might

be the spark to light an unseen fuse.
'I felt my waters break, contractions start,'

she says, 'two months too soon.
The doctor came, delivered both.

One breathing just. One dead
already in the womb.' She closes

sudden like a clam. The kettle hisses
ever louder, clicks and fades. Calmly

she prepares the tea, pours
the steaming brew into a china cup,

in silence offers you
sugar, milk, a slice of gingerbread

spread thick with love, with gratitude
that you have understood

no more should be said.

*

She's eighty, your father
has been nursed and set to rest,

his memory settled, solid, steady
as the granite headstone

where his name's engraved.
His praises have been sung.

He was big-hearted and much loved;
she did not weep beside his grave.

You've never seen her cry. Not once
in all your life. As if her heart's

a tomb where pain and grief
are long-since sealed. Solidified.

Her duty's been to keep the living
fed and warm and safe from any harm

that long-suppressed emotions leaking
from her unhealed wounds might wreak.

'The twins I lost,' she says one day.
We're in the garden, planting bulbs,

small crocuses to flower in the spring.
Birdsong fills the chilling autumn air.

'It happened at my mother's house,
I was more than six months gone.

And mad with grief. My husband,
just a boy, buried in a foreign grave.

The doctor who delivered them,
he was a butcher of a man.'

Her trowel rasps the stony earth,
I strain to hear her speak.

'Stoke up the front room fire,'
he said, while I still lay in shock

at all I'd lost, at so much pain.
My mother did as she was told.

He took them both, both their tiny
baby forms, wrapped them

with placenta, bloodied umbilical cord
in old newsprint. Placed the tiny

bundles on that blazing home-made
pyre. Flames leaped and roared.

My mother thanked
and paid him at the door.'

*

Cracked as an egg, off her head, daft
as a full moon on a neap tide, away

with the fairies, flying with the banshees,
pale as a corpse

cavorting to death's door,
a skinny rattling skeleton bride...

... my father pieced the jagged jigsaw
of her broken soul, a girl

three times bereaved by war, took
her firmly by the hand, the heart,

led her from the underworld of loss,
of guilt where fires of sorrow rage,

where monsters prowl, bore her
in strong arms from the grasping

jaws of grief where wild things
howl and gnash their teeth –

there are many ways
to be a hero in a war.

*

When she dies at eighty-eight,
we find a cardboard box

neatly stored inside, some knitting,
air-force blue, a jumper for a man,

front and back complete,
on one smooth needle all the neat

small stitches of a sleeve, each piece
packed in almost seventy years ago

beside aborted dreams, the lingering
musty mothballed scent of her survivor's guilt.

Below the wool we find once more
her gold engagement ring,

its diamonds patterned like a flower,
her necklace of glass beads,

and other items new to us;
an Airman's Logbook

and a leather pouch; in her neat print,
his name inside its flap. On opening it

we find a briar pipe, his teeth marks
on the lip, and in its bowl

the tamped tobacco, cracked and black,
waiting for the man who

flew out in the dark
that summer evening 1944 –

*

Airman's Log. Final entry.

June 5th/6th. We are required tonight
and is nearly time for briefing
so I'll carry on when I get back

*

against the midnight sky
of Normandy
his life unravelled
in a final blazing
umbilical cord
of fear and flame

this box, my mother's
life-long shrine to him.

*

Slender, warm and oh so tall,
dove grey eyes, gentle hands,

film star beautiful, singing
Que sera, sera, and strong, so strong,

this is the mother we loved
and saw when we were small

in that house of ghosts and
sudden chills, of quiet sorrows

where soft white feathers
would suddenly drift down

land on windowsills,
that house of war-wounded

of war survivors,
where the stillborn

and the war dead
mingled in memory

crept into our dreams
watched over us silently

cast long shadows
as we played.

Slip into the Moment

slip into the moment
between dusk and dark

between the breathing in
and the breathing out

into the moment between
the thought and the word

the silence and the sound
the sob and the agony of loss

the ripple of pleasure and
the laugh

imagine stepping
from a dancing boat

onto the solid shore, imagine
that split second where

you are suspended in mid air –
imagine if just then a passer-by

taking a photo of the view beyond
the sparkling sea, the far horizon

the white clouds drifting – caught
you, not in the boat, not on the land

but suspended spirit-like, hovering
defying the weight of flesh

and blood and bone
slip into that moment if you can

slip into that moment if you dare
maybe that's the moment where

you'll find out who you really are

Burial Ground

In spring there is no need for sun,
daffodils turn granite gravestones gold.

Summer and a bee throbs in a head
of luscious clover. A mayfly twirls.

Tall daisies splash the shade with white.
A songthrush sashays through the grass,

two lizards dart out from a stack of rotting wood,
once a gate the living and the dead

passed through. The green-leafed branches of a tree,
solemn as pall-bearers, heft a blackened bough.

Beneath the mountain of light, bones shift quietly
under lime green lichened quilts of stone,

while the river's living snake purls and swirls,
swallows itself, is reborn, reborn.

In Winter Sunshine

weathered headstones
of those we love
cast
the longest shadows

Winter Night

the sky noisy with traffic
as honking geese head home

caught in the moon's headlight

Winter Morning

fingers of sunlight
massage frost-numbed limbs

lcaf buds quickcn
in wooden wombs

Broody Hill

under last night's snowfall the hill sleeps,
conifers fluffed as feathers on a speckled hen

listen when the wind stills
hear her quiet clucking

Greylag Geese

the train I'm on speeds past

a mob of greylag geese

the train I'm on speeds past

spread their wings

the train I'm on speeds past

make little runs

the train I'm on speeds past

are left forever

the train I'm on speeds past

between earth and air

April 2020

A child's voice bounces through the open window
of the lockdown house next door. In our garden
tulips flounce scarlet hussy petticoats, daffodils
bounce out golden notes, a chaffinch chirrucks
in a willow tree, catkin buds burst yellow,
fat and merry, cherry trees blush pink as candy-floss.

No constant traffic roar nearby. No white contrails
of planes criss-cross the sky. A perfect spring!
But for the distant sound of siren wails
that drift from time to time, invisible ribbons
in the dangerous air. They catch us unaware,
bind round our throats, constrain us as we isolate

and wait, uncertain what each day will bring
in this exuberant, this strangely fearful spring.

Pandemonious

In the pandemic, poems escape
in droplets from the mouths

of panicked poets, congregate
in midge swarms, hatch

from cracked stanzas, multiply
in fevered metaphors, proliferate

in the brains of the afflicted,
buzz onto our laptop screens

in zillions, worm into our ears,
explode like a rash from trillions

of poetry podcasts. Even the news
gets in on the act; a poem to help

you through. Too few precautions
are taken too late. Sufferers report

metaphor overload; asphyxiation
by alliteration; pun poisoning.

Stricken, they cough up rhyming couplets.
Gasp out ghazals. Vomit villanelles.

Listen, people! Death and suffering
by pandemic poem are avoidable!

Try earplugs. Blindfolds. Shoving
your head in a plain brown bag.

Or stand outside each night at eight
shout *STOP! No more! No more!*

Or isolate, all media off. And... wait.
The market says that soon enough

this rush to versify will dissipate.
There is no profit in it.

On the Hospice End of Life Ward

There's a window in the slanting roof
above the beds where the patients lie.

The sky flits slowly past; a gallery
of ever-changing photographs.

Watch as a perfect sheet of blue
shifts to a blur of stormy tears.

Doze off to a blank of boring grey.
Wake to a silver moon as it ghostly

trails thin veils of cloud across the dark.
Some say that on windless nights

when the sky is clear and deep,
you might even see heaven,

and drifting off to sleep, might
hear the voices of angels

talking softly by the nurses' station.

Missing

For MF

Her boots go with him
everywhere, in a zipped
Adidas shoulder bag.
A red leather ankle pair
she loved to wear, even
when the cancer
was walking her away.

They travel now on trains
and planes to places she will
never see. Once there, he finds
a spot, arranges them before
the view, and with the camera
she loved, he documents
her aching absence in his world.

At Ground Zero they pose
solemnly. In Sydney, sunshine
spotlights them
like starlets on the steps
before the Opera House. See!
At a magic finger-click they look
as if they might dance off,
high-kicking in their harlot-scarlet
glory for the hell of it.

But now, at sunset on the darkening sand
at Bantry Bay, they linger
by the lapping water's edge
as he recounts the day

she begged he help her
from her sterile clinic bed
so she could buy them –
hand-tooled Spanish leather
red-blooded as her gypsy soul
with Cuban heels that
clicked and clacked, and how
she wore them straight away,
even though with swollen
legs and chemo cocktails
coursing through her veins, her
brain, she could barely stand,
but swayed. *Ravaged*
and wrecked
and beautiful, he says.

Do you think I'm strange,
he asks as gently he slips
a hand inside each one,
where faint prints
of her toes are stained,
where traces
of her cells
remain.

If only the world were full
of such strangeness, I reply.
If only the world
were full of such love.

She Dares To Walk Where

1.

That spring there was an unexpected heat.
He met her in the coolness of De Courcey's,
bent his head, pecked her cheek,
wished her Happy Anniversary.

Crisp white tablecloth, white as an altar cloth,
white as a wedding dress, white as a shroud.
Salt in silver salvers, knives shining sharp.

He ordered for them both by flickering candlelight,
filled her glass with wine, a deep blood red.

You're not happy – quite suddenly – he said.
She moved her hand in fright
at his clear-sightedness, at her transparency.

The wine glass tipped, toppled, spilled,
bled across the snowy cotton of her dress,
stained her from breast to pubic bone,
a livid red.

2.

Was it her fault he never tired of her?
Always trying so hard. All sugar, all spice.
What could he do but love his little wife?
Always smiling, always nice.

3.

Mother, why did you not warn? Why
did you preach, why did you teach
a woman's one and only duty was to please?

What was it you said,
years after her father died?
I married a man I did not love,
you said with pride,
and in the course of fifty years
I learned to love, learned
contentment by his side.

Mother, that lie you swallowed
as a virgin bride all those years ago,
did it choke your voice so
you could never tell your daughter,
yes, she had a choice?

It's taken her a hundred years –
poor princess fed a poisoned apple –
a hundred years to wake,
the lie still bitter-green upon her tongue.

Now she's locked in a pretty glass coffin,
with its fitted kitchen and its bright conservatory.
Locked up in all her finery.

And the briars have climbed around the walls
the prince has toiled to build for her. The weeds
have multiplied like lies and choked the doors.
The love they grew to keep them safe,
like ivy, twines around them both,
cuts deeper as they grow – and won't let go.

4.

Early summer came on hot, and what he called
her madness blossomed in the damp, heavy heat.

She felt it like a quickening, as if a seed of discontent,
long dormant in the hard shell of her heart,
had split and swift began to germinate.

One day, he came in from the garden. Oh, how
she'd begged him cut the briars back!
They're stealing all the air, she said. *I cannot breathe.*

And now they lay in withering piles around the lawns.

He, damp with sweat, wiped his brow, said, *Princess,
how are you now?* She turned away. She could not speak,
her voice trapped in the locked cage of her throat –
and she had long since lost the key.

You need to see a doctor, he said quietly.
She bridled at his words, yet knew
he thought this was a caring thing to do.

5.

One day she read this in a book: cactus plants adapt to desert conditions. *They are trees, really. Their stumpy bodies trunks which store what little moisture comes their way. The spines and spikes are stunted leaves. Sometimes a cactus plant waits fifty years before it knows a glorious flowering.*

6.

Because her feet are cold she cannot sleep.
She lies on her side of the bed, her body stiff
and straight, for if she curls, surely he will spoon
around her foetus form, close like a shell
around a grain of sand, hoping when he wakes
she'll be a pearl again.

She shifts a little, rubs her feet one against the other.
Ice on ice. He turns and slips an arm around her waist.
She tries to breathe as if asleep. Plays dead. Smothers
the urge to rise and run away.

Out in the dark the warm winds gust the trees,
leaves wag like old wives' tongues,
throw curses at the leering moon.

The howl of a fox startles. And she recalls
the male fox screams
after he has fucked the vixen.
After he has spent his seed
her muscles spasm, hold him tight –

She lies awake, listens to the endless night.
Deep inside she knows – there's always one
who won't let go.

7.

The doctor's room is cheery, bright
with a castor oil plant – Palma Christi –
waving dark green hands to welcome her.

I've not been sleeping well, she says,
her voice so small
she hardly hears its whisper fall.

His eyebrows raise to question marks.

My feet are cold. Especially at night.
So cold I think I must be dead.

The doctor has a husband's face,
intelligent, reliable, kind.

You're forty-five, he says. She nods.
He shakes his head and sighs.

Any other symptoms? he enquires,
his voice so strange, as if it floats
through mists from centuries away.

Yes, she yearns to say. *I have this urge*
at night, to run away, to knot
the bed sheets tight
into a long white rope,
sling it from the window, shimmy down
and lope off barefoot
through the woods, howl
naked at the moon.

Instead, she softly shakes her head.

He shuts her file, suggests she gets out more,
try flower arranging, like his wife. Meanwhile,
he recommends she wear warm socks in bed.

8.

While her husband sleeps she creeps up to the loft,
thick with spider webs, the baby cot, dead moths,
the children's toys, the flotsam of their past.

She digs the album from a dust-thick shelf, sits
and flicks through photographs – a young bride,
smiling in a crisp white dress, white
as an altar cloth, white as a shroud.

Oh, what dreams she clutched
with his strong hand
and that bouquet of flowers...

Remember how her mother wept!
It's meant to be a happy day, her father sighed.
God knows, you'd think to see you weep, someone
had died.

She lingers on each photograph, stares
into a child's eyes,
so bright, brimful with hope, so wide

as the church organ sounds
Here comes the
Here comes the
Here comes the...

9.

How can I make you happy, he says.

She drains potatoes at the kitchen sink,
steam billows, scalds her face,
creamy water streams. Red-eyed,
she blinks and turns away.

I need to know, he says.

She holds the pan lid tight.
The window blossoms clouds,
blurs the garden and its trees.

And she would gladly answer –
if she but knew
what answer she could give.

The door slams as he leaves.

10.

Sometimes at dusk she walks
by the canal in airless heat,
the water dark and filmed with dust.

She stops and stares at shapes that lurk below:
clumps of brooding weed,
a tight-tied sack, water rats, imagines suicides,
the drowned detritus of broken lives.

She longs for the wildness of a mountain stream,
clear and gurgling, bubbling wildly, frothing,
clattering freely over stones and down ravines,
for a savage highland river, tawny water
tumbling laughing over rocks.

11.

I want to get a job, she says.

He smiles benignly. *What's the point in that?*
You're always saying you're tired. And anyway,
anything you want to buy is yours, my sweet.
Just ask.

12.

He buys her pretty things
to make her smile:
diamond-studded bracelets
he clips around her wrists,
a fine gold chain he fastens
round her neck.
He says they're symbols of his love

but the chain, though fine
as baby's hair, makes her choke

and every winking diamond
seems a watchful eye,
a tiny spy, he's paid
to track her every move.

13.

You shouldn't walk alone, he says. *It isn't safe,*
out there along the wooded paths.

She thinks of rapists stalking wives,
of murderers with glinting knives –

and wonders that he's unaware
the demons she most dreads
prowl constantly inside her head.

14.

The heat intensifies and discontent
grips vine-like tendrils at her throat.

She hears its green tongues hiss
inanities into her ear. *Go on girl,*
have some fun,
let down your hair. A bit adultery
– discreet – will hurt no-one.

Other times they scold, they taunt,
You really should appreciate your life,
you don't deserve this lovely house, this man
who gives you everything a wife could want.

15.

Today the sky is heavy, grey.
She walks by the canal, stands
upon the towpath, by the lock.
The water lies grave-still.

She stares into the deep. Wills
herself to take
one step, and then another, let
her body fall
down and down
and drown in liquid sleep.

16.

He knows she's still awake. He turns.
His hand slides up beneath the cotton
of her thin nightdress, slides warm
against her thigh, her breast.

He touches her. Is gentle. Whispering pleads.

She wants to please. She lets him stroke,
lets him kiss, lets him caress,
lets him enter her.

And in the blackness lies.
And in the silence, weeps.

17.

Sometimes she dares herself to walk too far, to where
the traffic noises fade, where thistles, parched and dry
grow shoulder-high, where nettles stretch across and bar
the way, where rosehips wink like whores
amongst the thorns, and red-rimmed eyes
of summer brambles stare.

18.

He's been out hunting while she slept.
A deer hangs in the shed, its brown eyes
wide and glazed. He's gralloched it,
tossed the steaming entrails to the dogs.
Red-muzzled, sated, now they laze.

He cleans his knife against the grass.
Blood stains his hands and clothes.

Once, she recalls, he said her eyes
were soft and gentle as a doe's.

19.

Her mother comes for Sunday tea.
She thinks he asked her here.
She sees them through a window
fringed with coils of waxed green hearts
and spider webs. They chat
together, stroll the garden paths, inspect
the walls he's newly built, frown
at the flowers' drooping necks,
complain the heat's too much,
we're needing rain.

She sits inside, staring at
a butterfly
fluttering paper wings
fluttering paper wings
fluttering paper wings
hopelessly
against the pane.

20.

Is there another man, he says.
All those walks by the canal…

She turns away and frowns.
I like to walk, that's all.

21.

His anger is contained. It seethes beneath
the thin set of his mouth, the tautened skin
upon his face, the shoulder muscles tensed,
the rigid line of spine.

She tippy-toes around, speaks seldom, wary
that each word is snatched upon, dissected,
inspected, its entrails spread, interpreted,

as if within the gristle and the guts and blood
of stringy consonants and disemboweled
vowels he'll find some remnant of the girl
he thinks that she should be.

22.

She is becoming secretive, fugitive.
She keeps her words locked tight away,
like a child with its favourite sweets,
a miser with his gold. She hides

books. Between their covers
her eyes have strayed –
she might have left traces, faint
as spider tracks in dust
of her deepest thoughts. Soon
she will need to wear soft gloves
to open the windows of her mind.

A careless thumbprint might
incriminate. She must not write
things down, except on pages
carried deep inside, bound tight,
with skull and skin.

23.

He threatened her. Just once.
Waved the paper in her face,
thumped his fist upon his desk,
made her read the headline

HUSBAND AXES WIFE TO DEATH

This is what you'll drive me to.
That's all he said.

24.

How many ways are there to leave a husband?
You could go out screaming, plates and glasses
smashing off the walls.

Or weeping quietly, trying not to
wake the street, determined not to brawl.

Or creep out in the dark of night, clutching
a polybag with your future and your toothbrush
and your broken dreams inside.

Or violently. Throw yourself, like Deirdre of the Sorrows,
from his speeding car.

Or take yourself out fast, steer 90 miles per hour
towards a roadside tree.

You could even go a-p-o-l-o-g-e-t-i-c-a-l-l-y,
blurting, *I know, it's all my fault!*

I hope one day you'll find the grace to pardon me.
You could go with a flounce, with a flurry,

in a blaze of indignation, in an unholy hurry.
Or you could just go. One day. When he's out.

Simply.   Place.   One
foot   in front of   the other...

Fear

stand alone

in a tunnel of firs
while the sun's burning

rage is swallowed
by the darkening

fringe of trees
brushing the sky

like eyes
softly closing

let darkness
circle, let

it stalk you
like a wolf

sense its hot breath
on your neck

don't move, don't

run
     run

          run
             run

                   ru

The First Recorded Case

The owner of the Highland Guesthouse
on the Banks of the Bonny Braes
– not a Scot by birth –
first dipped his toe, so claims his spouse,
as a marketing device, intended to entice
the tourists in. After all, he said, it works a treat
for oatcakes, rugs and haggises, for
Edinburgh Rock and sundry haberdasheries.

He started with the front lounge drapes,
a tasteful ancient Robertson.
Guests from the States were wowed.
Soon he'd papered every room,
each in a different clan – modern,
hunting, dress. Oh how he beamed
when guests from far Japan,
bowed down, impressed.

His wife hoped it would stop right there.
But no! What better, he declared,
than tartan carpet underfoot on every floor
and stair? And when soft furnishings
failed to satisfy – he turned, as addicts do –
to clothes and yes, to underwear.

He couldn't see himself
in what he called a man-skirt,
but tartan trews to match
the dining room would do the trick.
Seamlessly he slid from
harmless predilection to
full hard-core addiction.

Until, one night, his wife, off-season,
knitting tammies in the lounge,
disquieted by a muffled sound,
looked round and to her horror saw,
hovering disembodied,
(against the Clan Macgregor Ancient Dress)
her husband's pale moon face,
his startled hair, his look of quiet distress
as by an act of quiet transubstantiation
he morphed into half man, half tartan chair.

George Square, September 2014

A still September evening, we spill
from Queen Street Station, down
sun-streaked steps to George Square,

where sad clumps of lads and lassies
wreathed in Saltires and tartan
sit scattered like wilting blooms

on the grave of their dream
of a better nation. One boy strums
a battered guitar, plastered with stickers

curled at the edges, *Yes We Can*,
Forever Aye, Saor Alba.
In tiny kilts and tammies, girls

with tear-stained faces hug and hum along,
when suddenly the air vibrates, a cavalcade
of honking horns, a roisterous parade

of cars and vans comes revving up
from Cochrane Street, in a flap of Union Jacks
as big as sheets. Shouts and yells crack the air.

A crowd on foot invades the square
as if someone unseen somewhere
has fired a starting gun.

Mums, dads, grannies all come streaming in.
Babies in buggies waving tiny flags. And lo!
Britannia herself! Breasts high in a scarlet bra,

a swirling skirl of ribbons, red, white, blue,
birling round her spray-tanned thighs. And
women, waving voddie bottles, singing

like a choir of Furies
Ye can stick yer independence up yer arse!
while trickling through their midst,

young bloods, cans in fists, unfurling
Union Jacks, the Red Hand of Ulster,
the Cross of St George.

The early evening sun's still bright, but
shadows fall across us, cast a chill.
We stand stock still. Yet feel as if

we're slowly sliding somewhere
we don't want to go.
Fists punch the air. The referendum

victory's theirs and now they want the square.
But is that all? Men swarm around
a statue, clamber up its sides,

their neck veins bulge, forearms thrust,
faces gargoyle as they form a seething mass
Rule Britannia, Britannia Rules the Waves.

Capricious as cells splintering
from a cancer clump, random as sparks
from a raging blaze, some lads split

from its seething edge. One singles out
a kilted lass, spits in her face, struts off,
pleased as a playground thug. Another

shoves a blonde girl to the ground, wrests
her Saltire from her hand, sneers at his mate,
sets the flag alight. They laugh.

The 'Yes' kids don't retaliate.
Defiantly they sing their Flower of Scotland
requiem, mill around, confused.

Union families drift off home,
robbed of their celebration by their own.
Police arrive on horseback. Define a thin

blue line. A neo-fascist lights a flare. A flash
of luminescent green. Ejaculate of hate.
The hydra-headed gargoyle vents its spleen

in vomit flame and battle screams. And we
stand quietly, in the midst of all this madness,
wondering: Are these the Unionists who won

the vote? Or simply fascists spoiling for a fight?
These men who scream as if some primal
fear's been stamped into their brain at birth,

coded in their DNA, are they afraid that all they
have might suddenly be snatched away
if they don't fight! fight! fight!

Or is it boredom's pulled the pin
from the grenade
of thwarted masculinity?

Are they so tired of being bossed around,
being constantly ground down
by humdrum mind-numb jobs

they cannot stand?
While in this fascist brother-band
they find a place to flex their biceps,

beat their chests, wield a club, a gun,
a knife, an iron bar, a fist,
boast I Am Warrior!

Just then their voices rise as one –
God Save Our Gracious Queen!
The Hydra they've become roars and rears,

but makes no move to charge.
And we stand where we always will,
staring fascists down. Knowing them

for what they are. Little men
who measure out their lives
in lager cans of fear and hate,

desperate to be no longer small,
unheard, unseen.
No longer impotent and bored.

And just for this one moment,
not easily ignored.

Since You Left

my sorrow
is a bluebell
in a crystal glass

its head hangs heavy
its stem weakens
its petals shrivel

        my grief
        is a berry
        the brightest red

        within its scarlet skin
        sleep a million seeds
        a million tears
        i have yet to weep

my loneliness
is a water-lily
it floats on the surface of each day

with the waxed paleness
the musky scent of death
roots long
and lost in darkness

Dream Poetry Reading

Broke-back chairs, sticky floor, that
dingy bare-bulb back-room where
poets congregate late into the night
to incantate. Cloaked in a nervous grin,
I venture in, as if a smile could radiate
warmth and light. Men's eyes flick,
lizard-like, as I click-clack-click
across the floor, test a chair, hope it's
sound enough to bear my weight.

I know there's not much chance some
gulps of warm and vinegary white
will transubstantiate this dingy bar
in Glasgow, Inverness or Aberdeen,
to something more serene, but through
a high up window a harvest moon,
fat as a merry cow, is leaping a crowd
of silver-lined satanic clouds, and that jagged
ragged city skyline could be anywhere...

And sure enough, a half-glass later, I imagine
this is Greenwich Village, circa '66,
I'm clad in black, lighting a Gitane,
smoke drifts down in dreamy loops
above my head, I tip my chin up
Juliette Gréco style, and whoah!

in comes Ginsberg – naked – takes the mic,
This is the only way to read poetry, he says.

Time slips another decade, and
from the shadows Bukowski rises

from a battered sofa, sways across the floor,
a fat bee buzzing towards the honey jar
of my scarlet lips, but he's on the skids
of his own disappointments, and this
is my poem now, I'm holding the pen
and blue eyes or not, Bukowski's got
all the aura of a Jack-Daniels-soused
loser who's dossed once too often
in the mire of his own myths. Suddenly

time shifts once more and I'm back
in this here and now of piss
stained sofas and deflated dreams.

And I wonder if all the cool downtown bar
and cafe readings of the past
with their women with long slim
legs that poets eulogised, the ones
that opened with the automatic ease
of shiny doors in classy department stores
the minute the bards appeared purring
lines of off-beat beat-up
beat-you beat-me
beat to the beat-beat-beat –

Oh those women with breasts
so perfect for ripe-fruit metaphors!
If maybe all that was only ever
an urban poetry myth.

And all those nights were pretty much like
this, with the fat moon leaping
in the satanic sky and the broke-back
chairs, sticky floors, the terminally
depressed light bulbs, and

these thoughts are barreling
through my brain like a night train
on acid bound for hell on the seedy
side of the tracks when my name spits
and cracks from the faulty PA. I stub out
my fantasy in the soft grey ash
of reality, and minutes later I'm there

in the spotlight, making love
to the mic with image
and rhythm and rhyme
and I'm sure I hear the soft notes
of a saxophone, swimming up slow
from the street below
in lapping waves of blue
and I tell myself this,
this is for real, this is sublime,
this perfect poetry reading.
And I'm not faking it, no,
oh no, I'm not faking it,
not this time.

Notes on Poems

'Sitting for Joyce'
In May 2019 Joyce Gunn Cairns' exhibition of
portraits of Edinburgh Makars and several other
Scottish poets, including that of Magi Gibson, were
exhibited at the Scottish Poetry Library in Edinburgh.

'Kitchen Sink'
Margaret Watkins was born in Ontario, Canada in
1884 and died in Glasgow, Scotland in 1969. In the first
half of her life she was a commercial and innovative
photographer in New York. After coming to Glasgow in
1929 to visit her aunts she stayed on, though she always
planned to go back. In later decades her reputation as a
photographer was unknown to those in the city where
she lived quietly. In her 80s she entrusted a large brown
parcel to her Hyndland neighbour, Joe Mulholland,
to be opened only after her death. Joe, owner of the
Hidden Lane Gallery, then discovered a treasure trove of
photographs and negatives. He has exhibited much of
her work, including *The Kitchen Sink*, and in great part
thanks to his efforts, her art has now been celebrated in
her native Canada.

'Letter from the Asylum 1915'
Born in 1864 Camille Claudel grew up in a small
town outside Paris. Her dream was to be a sculptor,
and when her family moved to Paris when she was
a teen she studied art against her mother's wishes.
Auguste Rodin, more than twice her age, pursued
her, they became very involved, then he refused to
leave his partner. She achieved high praise as an
innovative sculptor, but after an abortion for Rodin's
child, things went from bad to worse, and by 1913

her brother had her committed to an asylum (within days of their father's death). Later, both an old friend from England who visited, and the Director of the Asylum, declared her sane, but under French law her brother, a playwright, held all the power. She died still incarcerated, still sane in 1943 at the age of 78, never having sculpted again.

'Dead Women Count'
In the UK Jean Hatchett does sponsored bike rides every week for women killed by men they know. Since 2013 Karen Ingala Smith has run the Counting Dead Women campaign in the UK. She also collaborated on The Femicide Census with Women's Aid.

'Slip into the Moment'
Commissioned poem for 7 Short Sails. An artistic response to London-based artist/photographer Jane Watt's photo-film *A Day in the Life* depicting a river and quay-side with split-second illusionary effects. Fribo, three musicians from Norway, England and Scotland composed music in response to the poem.

Stella Cartwright
Stella Cartwright, who became known as The Muse of Rose Street, was introduced by her father to the group of Edinburgh poets who frequented bars there in the 1950s and '60s. Several claimed to have been in love with her, and George Mackay Brown became engaged to her. She died alone and an alcoholic at the age of 47. None of the poets came to her funeral.

The Poets' Pub
A painting by Scottish artist Sandy Moffat of a group of the best known Scottish poets of the mid-20th century. Moffat assembled them as a group for artistic purposes.

Acknowledgements

I WOULD LIKE to thank the editors of the following
magazines and anthologies where some of these
poems were first published, sometimes in earlier
versions. *Poetry Salzburg Review, Glasgow Review
of Books, Chapman, Bella Caledonia, The Poets'
Republic, Poets' React, Other Terrain Journal (Issue
7), Scotia Extremis, The Darg: A Celebration of
Hamish Henderson, The Stinging Fly, Live Encounters
Poetry, Southbank Poetry, The Morning Star,
Backstory Journal (Australia), A Kist of Thistles;
Culture Matters Anthology, Postcards from Malthusia
(New Boots and Pantisocracies), Together Behind
Four Walls (Arkbound).* And the following who
commissioned poems: StAnza/Glasgow Women's
Library 2018; StAnza/ Hamish Henderson Centenary
2019; The Year of Transgressive Women 2018,
Scottish Poetry Library, Joyce Gunn Cairns Artist
Exhibition, 2019; Strathcarron Hospice, 50th
Anniversary Commemoration; 7 Short Sails Art
Project Scottish Poetry Library/ National Poetry Day
Postcard.

Bringing together a collection of poems into a
book is, of course, a team effort. I'd like to thank
Gavin MacDougall at Luath Press for believing in
me as a poet and offering so readily to publish this
follow-up collection to *Washing Hugh MacDiarmid's
Socks.*

Thanks too to the Luath team, especially Carrie
Hutchison and Jennie Renton, who between them
have been the midwives who transformed my
manuscript into the book you are now holding.

In my writing life I'm blessed with the friendship,
laughter and loyalty of Jenny Lindsay and Ali

Whitelock, two amazing fellow poets. I am grateful to them both for their support. If you don't know their work, I recommend you seek it out.

And finally my husband. He's my first reader, he fetches me endless pots of perfectly brewed Assam tea, he listens when I need to talk ideas through, he knows when not to say, wouldn't that work better as a sonnet?

Oh, and of course he makes me laugh. After all, he is a comedy novelist and consummate performer. Take a bow, Ian Macpherson.

Also published by **Luath Press**

Washing Hugh MacDiarmid's Socks
Magi Gibson
ISBN: 978-1-910745-86-1 paperback £7.99

A woman sunbathing on a demolition site in Bridgeton. Two women in a punch-up in Glasgow's West End. A young mother breast-feeding in an art gallery. A working man stepping off a tenement roof on a snowy morning. City streets. Country lanes. A letter to Sappho. A ticking off for Nietzsche. Not to mention Hugh MacDiarmid's dirty socks. Or that poem with the intriguing title, 'V****A'.

It catches all the qualities of Gibson's best writing. Metaphorically juxtaposing the skeletons in her cupboard with the ghosts in her attic Gibson is a joy to read. —Hayden Murphy, THE NATIONAL

Details of this and other books published by Luath Press can be found at:
www.luath.co.uk

Luath Press Limited

committed to publishing well written books worth reading

LUATH PRESS takes its name from Robert Burns, whose little collie Luath (*Gael.*, swift or nimble) tripped up Jean Armour at a wedding and gave him the chance to speak to the woman who was to be his wife and the abiding love of his life. Burns called one of the 'Twa Dogs' Luath after Cuchullin's hunting dog in Ossian's *Fingal*. Luath Press was established in 1981 in the heart of Burns country, and is now based a few steps up the road from Burns' first lodgings on Edinburgh's Royal Mile. Luath offers you distinctive writing with a hint of unexpected pleasures.

Most bookshops in the UK, the US, Canada, Australia, New Zealand and parts of Europe, either carry our books in stock or can order them for you. To order direct from us, please send a £sterling cheque, postal order, international money order or your credit card details (number, address of cardholder and expiry date) to us at the address below. Please add post and packing as follows: UK – £1.00 per delivery address; overseas surface mail – £2.50 per delivery address; overseas airmail – £3.50 for the first book to each delivery address, plus £1.00 for each additional book by airmail to the same address. If your order is a gift, we will happily enclose your card or message at no extra charge.

Luath Press Limited
543/2 Castlehill
The Royal Mile
Edinburgh EH1 2ND
Scotland
Telephone: +44 (0)131 225 4326 (24 hours)
Email: sales@luath.co.uk
Website: www.luath.co.uk